A Gift for God

A Gift for God

PRAYERS AND MEDITATIONS

Mother Teresa

of Calcutta

HarperSanFrancisco

An Imprint of HarperCollins*Publishers*

A GIFT FOR GOD: *Prayers and Meditations.* Copyright © 1996 by Mother Teresa Missionaries of Charity.

HarperCollins Web Site: http://www.harpercollins.com
HarperCollins®, 📖®, and HarperSanFrancisco™ are trademarks of HarperCollins Publishers Inc.

FIRST HARPERCOLLINS PAPERBACK EDITION PUBLISHED IN 1996
ISBN 0–06–068152–7 (pbk.)

Designed by Patricia Girvin Dunbar

An Earlier Edition of This Book Was Cataloged As Follows:
Teresa, Mother, 1910–
A Gift for God / Mother Teresa of Calcutta—1st U.S. edition, New York: Harper & Row, c1975.
1. Meditations. I. Title.
BX2182,2T39 1975   242'.4   76–351372
ISBN 0–06–068233–7

97 98 99 00 HAD 10 9 8 7 6 5 4 3

Contents

"I thirst."
John 19:28

A Gift for God

NO SLUMS IN HEAVEN

An Introduction
by Malcolm Muggeridge

This selection from the sayings, prayers, meditations, letters, and addresses of Mother Teresa will, it is hoped, serve to convey their style and flavor, as well as provide an acceptable manual of devotion for her admirers and followers. She is normally economical of words—as, indeed, of almost everything else except love and the worship of God—but when she uses them, whether spoken or written, they invariably come from the heart and are characteristically her own. She never, as far as is known, prepares beforehand what she proposes to say; apart, of course, from going to the chapel, where everything is prepared. Once, when she was waiting for a London bus, she was given a bunch of violets by a flower-seller who remembered seeing her on a TV program. She told me about this, adding: "We must give the flowers to Him." So I accompanied her to the chapel to lay them on the altar. It was one of those unforgettably exquisite incidents that buoy one up in this troubled world.

The force of her words is very great, as has been shown again and again before all sorts of audiences, from the most sophisticated to her own poorest of the poor. She makes no concession in the way of adjusting content or idiom to the ostensible IQ of her hearers; the message is always the same, yet always fresh and striking. Truth, in her shining version, can never be repetitive or banal, as its poor moralizing or pedantic image so often is. It is still remembered in Canada how, appearing on a TV program with Jacques Monod and Jean Vanier, she sat with her head seemingly bowed in prayer while the famous French molecular biologist and Nobel prize-winner animadverted upon how the whole future destiny of the human race is inexorably locked up in our genes. When pressed by the compère for her views, she simply lifted up her head and remarked: "I believe in love and compassion," then resumed her devotions. Her intervention, reinforcing Jean Vanier's powerful Christian testimony, was somehow decisive, and Professor Monod was afterwards heard saying that a little more of the same treatment and his sound atheistic position might be jeopardized.

On another occasion Mother Teresa made an appearance on one of those morning shows that help Americans to munch their breakfast cereal and swallow their coffee. It was the first time she had been in a New York TV studio, so she was unprepared for the constant interruptions for commercials. Also, the colors on the monitor screen, with her interlocutor appearing to have green hair, a mauve nose, and a drooping pink moustache, took her by surprise. As it happened, that particular morning the commercials were all about different varieties of packaged bread and other foods, commended to viewers as being nonfattening and nonnourishing. It took some little time for the irony to strike home, Mother Teresa's own constant preoccupation being, of course, to find the wherewithal to nourish the starving and put some flesh on human skeletons. When it did, she was heard to remark in a quiet but perfectly audible voice: "I see that Christ is needed in television studios." It was an unprecedented occurrence; a word of truth had been spoken in one of the mills of fantasy where the great twentieth-century myth of happiness successfully pursued is fabricated. A sudden silence descended on the studio, and it seemed as though the lights must go out and the floor-manager be struck dumb. Actually, as the commercials were still running, Mother Teresa was not on the air, and the impact of her interruption was soon spent. All the same, it surely rated a mention in the Book of Life, if not in the *New York Times.*

It is in her letters that the laughter which, with Mother Teresa, is never far away comes over most clearly—those letters, so wonderfully beautiful and wonderfully funny, that she writes late at night, or in trains and airplanes, always in her own hand and on the cheapest possible notepaper. One of the reasons that she so loves the poor is, I feel sure, that they laugh more than the rich, who are prone to excessive solemnity. Likewise power-maniacs of every stamp, who not only refrain from laughter themselves but hold it in abhorrence, like Shakespeare's King John finding it a passion hateful to their purposes. Not so Mother Teresa, who finds laughter very conducive to hers. A smiling face, she insists, is an integral part of Christian love, and her Missionaries of Charity are induced to make their houses ring with laughter as St. Francis and his friars laughed their way up and down the highways of the medieval world. In every saint there is a clown, and vice versa. What are saints, after all, but transcendental clowns, who, when the gates of heaven swing open, hear, mixed with the celestial music, celestial laughter? At the heart of the universe they find a mystery that is also a joke.

Thus, in a letter from Calcutta, Mother Teresa recalls how, in the early days of her work there, she was stricken with a high fever. "In that delirium," she writes, "I went to St. Peter, but he would not let me in, saying: 'There are no slums in heaven.' In my anger I said: 'Very well, I will fill heaven with slum people, then you will be forced to let me in.' Poor St. Peter! Since then the Sisters and Brothers don't give him rest, and he has to be so careful because our people have reserved their places in heaven long ago by their suffering. At the end they only had to get a ticket for St. Peter. All those thousands who have died with us have been given the joy of a ticket for St. Peter."

To a friend who is sorely ill and has asked for her prayers, she writes: "Your name is up on the wall, and the whole house will pray for you, including me. St. Peter will be surprised at the avalanche of prayer for you, and will, I am sure, make you well soon. Maybe, though, you are ready to go 'home' to God. If so, he will be very happy to open the 'door' for you and let you in for all eternity." Then, in her inimitable way, she adds: "If you go 'home' before me, give Jesus and his mother my love."

Again, apropos the opening of a Missionaries of Charity house in Lucknow, she writes: "You will be pleased to know that the heat this year has been really hot, so our Lucknow house was really founded on Burning Love. It is good to burn with the

8

heat of God outside since we don't burn with the heat of God in our hearts. . . . In Lucknow we get for our dwelling-place an old English cemetery, so if the Sisters start singing English songs at night you will know where it is coming from." As it happens, Mother Teresa brought a party of Sisters to visit my home, and while there they sang some English songs very sweetly, but they did not come, I swear, from the old Lucknow cemetery. I think I know where they came from, and trust that the following pages may contain echoes of the same singing and the same laughter that accompanied it.

LOVE BEGINS AT HOME

I think the world today is upside-down, and is suffering so much, because there is so very little love in the homes and in family life. We have no time for our children, we have no time for each other; there is no time to enjoy each other. If we could only bring back into our lives the life that Jesus, Mary, and Joseph lived in Nazareth, if we could make our homes another Nazareth, I think that peace and joy would reign in the world.

Love begins at home; love lives in homes, and that is why there is so much suffering and so much unhappiness in the world today. If we listen to Jesus he will tell us what he said before: "Love one another, as I have loved you." He has loved us through suffering, dying on the Cross for us, and so if we are to love one another, if we are to bring that love into life again, we have to begin at home.

We must make our homes centers of compassion and forgive endlessly.

Everybody today seems to be in such a terrible rush, anxious for greater developments and greater riches and so on, so that children have very little time for their parents. Parents have very little time for each other,

and in the home begins the disruption of the
peace of the world.

People who love each other fully and truly
—they are the happiest people in the world,
and we see that with our very poor people.
They love their children, and they love their
home. They may have very little, they may
have nothing, but they are happy people.

A living love hurts. Jesus, to prove his love
for us, died on the Cross. The mother, to
give birth to her child, has to suffer. If you
really love one another properly, there must
be sacrifice.

FAITH

I would be disposed to renounce my life rather than my faith.

Faith is a gift of God. Without it there would be no life. And our work, to be fruitful, and to be all for God, and to be beautiful, has to be built on faith—faith in Christ, who has said, "I was hungry, I was naked, I was sick, and I was homeless, and you ministered to me." On these words of his all our work is based.

Faith is lacking because there is so much selfishness and so much gain only for self. But faith, to be true, has to be a giving love. Love and faith go together. They complete each other.

I think, dear friend, I understand you better now. I am afraid I could not answer to your deep suffering. I don't know why, but you to me are like Nicodemus, and I am sure the answer is the same—"Unless you become a little child . . ." I am sure you will understand beautifully everything—if you would only become a little child in God's hands. Your longing for God is so deep, and yet he keeps himself away from you. He must be forcing himself to do so, because he loves you so much as to give Jesus to die for you and for me. Christ is longing to be your

Food. Surrounded with fullness of living Food, you allow yourself to starve. The personal love Christ has for you is infinite—the small difficulty you have regarding the Church is finite. Overcome the finite with the infinite. Christ created you because he wanted you. I know what you feel—terrible longing, with dark emptiness—and yet, he is the one in love with you. I do not know if you have seen these few lines before, but they fill and empty me:

My God, my God, what is a heart
That thou should'st so eye and woo,
Pouring upon it all thy heart
As if thou hadst nothing else to do?

Today what is happening on the surface of the Church will pass. For Christ, the Church is the same today, yesterday and tomorrow. The Apostles went through the same feelings of fear and distrust, failure and disloyalty, and yet Christ did not scold them—just "Little children, little faith, why did you fear?" I wish we could love as he did—*now.*

SUFFERING

Suffering is increasing in the world today. People are hungry for something more beautiful, for something greater than people round about can give. There is a great hunger for God in the world today. Everywhere there is much suffering, but there is also great hunger for God and love for each other.

There is hunger for ordinary bread, and there is hunger for love, for kindness, for thoughtfulness; and this is the great poverty that makes people suffer so much.

Suffering in itself is nothing; but suffering shared with Christ's passion is a wonderful gift. Man's most beautiful gift is that he can share in the passion of Christ. Yes, a gift and a sign of his love; because this is how his Father proved that he loved the world— by giving his Son to die for us.

And so in Christ it was proved that the greatest gift is love: because suffering was how he paid for sin.

Without him we could do nothing. And it is at the altar that we meet our suffering poor. And in him that we see that suffering can become a means to greater love and greater generosity.

Without our suffering, our work would just be social work, very good and helpful, but not the work of Jesus Christ, not part of the Redemption. Jesus wanted to help by sharing our life, our loneliness, our agony, our death. Only by being one with us has he redeemed us.

We are asked to do the same; all the desolation of the poor people, not only their material poverty, but their spiritual destitution, must be redeemed. And we must share it, for only by being one with them can we redeem them by bringing God into their lives and bringing them to God.

Suffering, if it is accepted together, borne together, is joy.

Amongst our Co-Workers we have sick and

crippled people who very often cannot do anything to share in the work. So they adopt a Sister or a Brother, offering all their sufferings and all their prayers for that Brother or that Sister, who then involves the sick Co-Worker fully in whatever he or she does. The two become like one person, and they call each other their second self. I have a second self like this in Belgium, and when I was last there she said to me: "I am sure you are going to have a heavy time, with all the walking and working and talking. I know this from the pain I have in my spine, and the very painful operation which I shall shortly need to have." That is her seventeenth operation, and each time that I have something special to do, it is she behind me that gives me all the strength and courage to do what I have to do to fulfill God's will. This is why I am able to do what

22

I am doing; as my second self, she does all the most difficult part of the work for me.

My very dear suffering sisters and brothers, be assured that every one of us claims your love before the throne of God, and there every day we offer you, or rather offer each other, to Christ for souls. We, the Missionaries of Charity, how grateful we must be —you to suffer and we to work. We complete in each other what is lacking in our relationship with Christ. Your life of sacrifice is the chalice, or rather our vows are the chalice, and your suffering and our work are the wine—the spotless heart. We stand together holding the same chalice, and so are able to satiate his burning thirst for souls.

I find the work much easier and I can smile

more sincerely when I think of each one of my suffering brothers and sisters. Jesus needs you to keep pouring into the lamp of our life the oil of your love and sacrifice. You are really reliving the passion of Christ. Bruised, divided, full of pain and wounds as you are, accept Jesus as he comes into your life.

If sometimes our poor people have had to die of starvation, it is not because God didn't care for them, but because you and I didn't give, were not instruments of love in the hands of God, to give them that bread, to give them that clothing; because we did not recognize him, when once more Christ came in distressing disguise—in the hungry man, in the lonely man, in the homeless child, and seeking for shelter.

God has identified himself with the hungry, the sick, the naked, the homeless; hunger, not only for bread, but for love, for care, to be somebody to someone; nakedness, not of clothing only, but nakedness of that compassion that very few people give to the unknown; homelessness, not only just for a shelter made of stone, but that homelessness that comes from having no one to call your own.

IMITATION OF CHRIST

My very dear children, let us love Jesus with our whole heart and soul. Keep smiling. Smile at Jesus in your suffering—for to be a real Missionary of Charity you must be a cheerful sufferer. How happy I am to have you all; you belong to me as much as every Sister belongs to me here. And often when the work is very hard I think of each one of you, and tell God: "Look at my suffering children, and for their love bless this work." The response is immediate. So you see, you are our treasure-house—the power-house of the Missionaries of Charity.

Because we cannot see Christ we cannot express our love to him; but our neighbors we can always see, and we can do for them what, if we saw him, we would like to do for Christ.

Today, the same Christ is in people who are unwanted, unemployed, uncared for, hungry, naked, and homeless. They seem useless to the state and to society; nobody has time for them. It is you and I as Christians, worthy of the love of Christ if our love is true, who must find them, and help them; they are there for the finding.

There is always the danger that we may just do the work for the sake of the work.

This is where the respect and the love and the devotion come in—that we do it for God, for Christ, and that's why we try to do it as beautifully as possible.

Christians stand as the light for the others . . . for the people in the world. If we are Christians then we must be Christlike.

If you learn this art of being thoughtful, you will become more and more Christlike, for his heart was meek and he always thought of others. Thoughtfulness is the beginning of great sanctity. Our vocation, to be beautiful, must be full of thought for others. Jesus went about doing good. Our Lady in Cana only thought of the needs of others and made their needs known to Jesus.

A Christian is a tabernacle of the living God. He created me, he chose me, he came to dwell in me, because he wanted me. Now that you have known how much God is in love with you, it is but natural that you spend the rest of your life radiating that love.

To be a true Christian means the true acceptance of Christ, and the becoming of another Christ one to another. To love as we are loved, and as Christ has loved us from the Cross, we have to love each other and give to others.

When Christ said: "I was hungry and you fed me," he didn't mean only the hunger for bread and for food; he also meant the hunger to be loved. Jesus himself experienced this loneliness. He came amongst his own and his own received him not, and it hurt him then and it has kept on hurting him. The same hunger, the same loneliness, the same having no one to be accepted by and to be loved and wanted by. Every human being in that case resembles Christ in his loneliness; and that is the hardest part, that's real hunger.

CARRIERS OF CHRIST'S LOVE

Let us from the beginning try to live the spirit of the Missionaries of Charity, which is one of total surrender to God, loving trust in each other, and cheerfulness with all. If we really accept this spirit, then, for sure, we will be the true Co-Workers of Christ—the carriers of his love. This spirit must radiate from your own heart to your family, neighbor, town, country, the world. Let us more and more insist on raising funds of love, of kindness, of understanding, of peace. Money will come if we seek first the Kingdom of God; the rest will be given.

I would rather make mistakes in kindness and compassion than work miracles in unkindness and hardness.

We know that if we really want to love we must learn how to forgive.

We would not be able to understand and effectively help those who lack all, if we did not live like them. All gestures of love, however small they be, in favor of the poor and the unwanted, are important to Jesus.

Do not wait for leaders; do it alone, person to person.

As each Sister is to become a Co-Worker of

Christ in the slums, each ought to understand what God and the Missionaries of Charity expect from her. Let Christ radiate and live his life in her and through her in the slums. Let the poor, seeing her, be drawn to Christ and invite him to enter their homes and their lives. Let the sick and suffering find in her a real angel of comfort and consolation. Let the little ones of the streets cling to her because she reminds them of him, the friend of the little ones.

Our life of poverty is as necessary as the work itself. Only in heaven will we see how much we owe to the poor for helping us to love God better because of them.

Our lives are woven with Jesus in the Eucharist, and the faith and the love that come from the Eucharist enable us to see him in the distressing disguise of the poor, and so there is but one love of Jesus, as there is but one person in the poor—Jesus. We take vows of chastity to love Christ with undivided love; to be able to love him with undivided love we take a vow of poverty that frees us from all material possessions, and with that freedom we can love him with undivided love, and from this vow of undivided love we surrender ourselves totally to him in the person who takes his place. So our vow of obedience is another way of giving, of being loved. And the fourth vow that we take is to give wholehearted free service to the poorest of the poor. By this vow, we bind ourselves to be one of them, to depend solely on divine providence, to have nothing, yet possess all things in possessing Christ.

Let there be no pride or vanity in the work.

The work is God's work, the poor are God's poor. Put yourself completely under the influence of Jesus, so that he may think his thoughts in your mind, do his work through your hands, for you will be all-powerful with him to strengthen you.

Make sure that you let God's grace work in your souls by accepting whatever he gives you, and giving him whatever he takes from you. True holiness consists in doing God's will with a smile.

God is purity himself; nothing impure can come before him, but I don't think God can hate, because God is love and God loves us in spite of our misery and sinfulness. He is our loving Father and so we have only to turn to him. God cannot hate; God loves because he is love, but impurity is an obstacle to seeing

God. This doesn't mean only the sin of impurity, but any attachment, anything that takes us away from God, anything that makes us less Christlike, any hatred, any uncharitableness is also impurity. If we are full of sin, God cannot fill us, because even God himself cannot fill what is full. That's why we need forgiveness to become empty, and then God fills us with himself.

Co-Workers should give love in action. Our works of love are nothing but works of peace. Let us do them with greater love and efficiency, each in his or her own work, in daily life, at home, with one's neighbor.

Keep giving Jesus to your people, not by words, but by your example, by your being in love with Jesus, by radiating his holiness and spreading his fragrance of love everywhere you go. Just keep the joy of Jesus as your strength. Be happy and at peace. Accept whatever he gives—and give whatever he takes with a big smile. You belong to him. Tell him: "I am yours, and if you cut me to pieces, every single piece will be only all yours." Let Jesus be the victim and the priest in you.

Actually we are touching Christ's body in the poor. In the poor it is the hungry Christ that we are feeding, it is the naked Christ that we are clothing, it is to the homeless Christ that we are giving shelter.

It is not just hunger for bread or the need of the naked for clothes or of the homeless for a house made of bricks. Even the rich are hungry for love, for being cared for, for being wanted, for having someone to call their own.

❖

Jesus Christ has said that we are much more important to his Father than the grass, the birds, the flowers of the earth; and so, if he takes such care of these things, how much more would he take care of his life in us. He cannot deceive us; because life is God's greatest gift to human beings. Since it is created in the image of God, it belongs to him; and we have no right to destroy it.

❖

We ourselves feel that what we are doing is just a drop in the ocean. But if that drop was not in the ocean, I think the ocean would be less because of that missing drop. I do not agree with the big way of doing things. To us what matters is an individual. To get to love the person we must come in close contact with him. If we wait till we get the numbers, then we will be lost in the numbers. And we will never be able to show that love and respect for the person. I believe in person to person; every person is Christ for me, and since there is only one Jesus, that person is the one person in the world at that moment.

Let us try more and more to make every Sister, Brother, and Co-Worker grow into the likeness of Christ, to allow him to live his life of compassion and humanity in the world of today. Your love for Christ must be great. Keep the light of Christ always burning in your heart, for he alone is the Way to walk. He is the Life to live. He is the Love to love.

There is always the danger that we may become only social workers, or just do the work for the sake of the work. It is a danger if we forget to whom we are doing it. Our works are only an expression of our love for Christ. Our hearts need to be full of love for him, and since we have to express that love in action, naturally then the poorest of the poor are the means of expressing our love for God. . . . A Hindu gentleman said that they and we are doing social work, and the difference between them and us is that they are doing it for something, and we are doing it for Somebody.

This experience which we have by serving them, we must pass on to people who have not had that beautiful experience. It is one of the great rewards of our work.

If there are people who feel that God wants them to change the structures of society, that is something between them and their

God. We must serve him in whatever way we are called. I am called to help the individual; to love each poor person. Not to deal with institutions. I am in no position to judge.

Publicity I don't need. No, no, I do not need it. God's work has to be done in his own way; and he has his own ways and means of making our work known. See what has happened throughout the world and how the Sisters have been accepted in places where nobody ever knew anything about them. They have been accepted where many other people find it difficult to live or to be. So I think this is God himself proving that it is his work.

Be kind and merciful. Let no one ever come to you without leaving better and happier.

Be the living expression of God's kindness; kindness in your face, kindness in your eyes, kindness in your smile, kindness in your warm greeting. In the slums we are the light of God's kindness to the poor. To children, to the poor, to all who suffer and are lonely, give always a happy smile. Give them not only your care, but also your heart.

A smile must always be on our lips for any child to whom we offer help, for any to whom we give companionship or medicine. It would be very wrong to offer only our cures; we must offer to all our heart. Government agencies accomplish many things in the field of assistance. We must offer something else: Christ's love.

There should be less talk; a preaching point

is not a meeting point. What do you do then?
Take a broom and clean someone's house.
That says enough.

All of us are but his instruments, who do
our little bit and pass by.

OUR LADY

Mary is the mother of God, mother of Jesus and our mother, mother of the Church.

She is the mother of the whole world because when the angel gave her the news, the good news, that she would become the mother of Christ, it was at that time, by accepting to become the handmaid of the Lord, that she accepted to be our mother also, for the whole of mankind. Mother Mary is the hope of mankind.

She has given us Jesus. By joyously becoming his mother she became the mediatress in the salvation of mankind.

At the foot of the Cross she became our mother also, because Jesus said when he was dying that he gave his mother to St. John and St. John to his mother. At that moment we became her children.

The most beautiful part of our Lady was that when Jesus came into her life, immediately, in haste, she went to St. Elizabeth's place to give Jesus to her and to her son. And we read in the Gospel that the child "leapt with joy" at this first contact with Christ.

I think that if Jesus was able to listen to our

Lady, we should be able to listen to him also. At the Cross we find her sharing with Christ in his passion. Again and again she comes into our lives, into the life of the world, to bring joy and peace. To lead us back to God.

I am only a small instrument in God's hand. Our Lord and our Lady gave all the glory to God the Father; like them, in a very, very small way, I want to give all the glory to God the Father.

Let us ask our Lady to make our hearts "meek and humble" as her Son's was. It is so very easy to be proud and harsh and selfish—so easy; but we have been created for greater things. How much we can learn from our Lady! She was so humble because she was all for God. She was full of grace.

49

Tell our Lady to tell Jesus: "They have no wine; they need the wine of humility and meekness, of kindness and sweetness." She is sure to tell us, "Do whatever he tells you."

RICHES

Let us not be satisfied with just giving money; money is not enough, for money one can get. The poor need our hands to serve them, they need our hearts to love them. The religion of Christ is love, the spreading of love.

There must be a reason why some people can afford to live well. They must have worked for it. I only feel angry when I see waste. When I see people throwing away things that we could use.

The trouble is that rich people, well-to-do people, very often don't really know who the poor are; and that is why we can forgive them, for knowledge can only lead to love, and love to service. And so, if they are not touched by the poor, it's because they do not know them.

I try to give to the poor people for love what the rich could get for money. No, I wouldn't touch a leper for a thousand pounds; yet I willingly cure him for the love of God.

A GEOGRAPHY OF COMPASSION

There is no great difference in reality between one country and another, because it is always people you meet everywhere. They may look different or be dressed differently, they may have a different education or position; but they are all the same. They are all people to be loved; they are all hungry for love.

I feel Indian to the most profound depths of my soul.

The sari allows the Sisters to feel poor amongst the poor, to identify themselves with the sick, with the children, with the old and destitute. The Missionaries of Charity share, in their way of dressing, the way of life of the poorest in this world. Of course, India needs technicians, skilled men, economists, doctors, nurses, for her development. She needs plans and a general coordinated action. But how long would we have to wait for those plans to produce results? We do not know. Meanwhile, the people have to live, they have to be given food to eat, to be taken care of and dressed. Our field of action is the present India. While these needs continue, our work will continue.

We picked up a young man from the streets of Calcutta. He was very highly educated and had many degrees. He had fallen into bad hands and had his passport stolen. After some time I asked him why he had left home. He said his father did not want him. "From childhood he never looked me in the eyes. He became jealous of me, so I left home." After much praying, the Sisters helped him to return home, to forgive his father, and this has helped both of them. This is a case of very great poverty.

Some weeks back I heard there was a family who had not eaten for some days—a Hindu family—so I took some rice and I went to the family. Before I knew where I was, the mother of the family had divided the rice into two and she took the other half to the next-door neighbors, who happened to be a Moslem family. Then I asked her: "How much will all of you have to share?

There are ten of you with that bit of rice."
The mother replied: "They have not eaten
either." This is greatness.

In Calcutta our Sisters and Brothers work
for the poorest of the poor, who aren't
wanted, aren't loved, are sick and die, for
the lepers and the little children, but I can
tell you I have never yet in these twenty-five
years heard a poor person grumble or curse
or feel miserable. I remember I picked up a
person from the street who was nearly
eaten up with maggots, and he said: "I have
lived like an animal in the street but I am
going to die like an angel, loved and cared
for." And he did die like an angel—a very
beautiful death.

A girl came from outside India to join the
Missionaries of Charity. We have a rule that

the very next day new arrivals must go to the Home for the Dying. So I told this girl: "You saw Father during Holy Mass, with what love and care he touched Jesus in the Host. Do the same when you go to the Home for the Dying, because it is the same Jesus you will find there in the broken bodies of our poor." And they went. After three hours the newcomer came back and said to me with a big smile—I have never seen a smile quite like that—"Mother, I have been touching the body of Christ for three hours." And I said to her: "How—what did you do?" She replied: "When we arrived there, they brought a man who had fallen into a drain, and been there for some time. He was covered with wounds and dirt and maggots, and I cleaned him and I knew I was touching the body of Christ."

Some people came to Calcutta, and before leaving, they begged me: "Tell us something that will help us to live our lives better." And I said: "Smile at each other; smile at your wife, smile at your husband, smile at your children, smile at each other—it doesn't matter who it is—and that will help you to grow up in greater love for each other." And then one of them asked me: "Are you married?" and I said: "Yes, and I find it difficult sometimes to smile at Jesus." And it is true, Jesus can be very demanding also, and it is at those times when he is so demanding that to give him a big smile is very beautiful.

Visiting our houses in India, I have a beautiful time with Jesus in the train.

The suffering in the refugee camps is great.

It all looks like one big Calvary, where Christ is crucified once more. Help is needed, but unless there is forgiveness, there will be no peace, and this is also true in Belfast and other strife-ridden places.

We have a home for homeless alcoholics in Melbourne, and one of the men was very badly hurt by another. I thought that this would be a case for the police, so we sent for them. A policeman came and asked this gentleman: "Who did that to you?" The man started telling all kinds of lies, but he wouldn't tell the truth; he wouldn't give the name. Then the policeman had to go away without doing anything. We asked the man: "Why did you not tell the police who did that to you?" And he looked at me and he said: "His suffering is not going to lessen my suffering." He hid the name of his brother to save him from suffering. How beautiful and how great is the love of our people, and this is a continual miracle of love that spreads amongst our poor people.

Some months back a man who had been beaten up was picked up from the streets of Melbourne. He was an alcoholic who had been for years in that state, and the Sisters took him to their Home of Compassion. From the way they touched him, the way they took care of him, suddenly it was clear to him: "God loves me!" He left the home and never touched alcohol again, and went back to his family, to his children, to his job. Later, when he got his first salary, he came to the Sisters and gave them the money, saying: "I want you to be for others the love of God, as you have been to me."

In a place in Melbourne I visited an old man who nobody seemed to know existed. I saw his room; it was in a terrible state. I wanted to clean it, but he kept on saying: "I'm all right." I didn't say a word, yet in the end he allowed me to clean his room.

There was in that room a beautiful lamp, covered for many years with dirt. I asked him: "Why do you not light the lamp?" "For whom?" he said. "No one comes to me; I do not need the lamp." I asked him: "Will you light the lamp if a Sister comes to see you?" He said: "Yes, if I hear a human voice, I will do it." The other day he sent me a word: "Tell my friend that the light she has lighted in my life is still burning."

The Sisters are doing the small things in

New York—helping the children, visiting the lonely, the sick, the unwanted. We know now that being unwanted is the greatest disease of all. That is the poverty we find around us here. In one of the houses where the Sisters visit, a woman living alone was dead many days before she was found, and she was found because her body had begun to decompose. The people around her did not know her name. When someone told me that the Sisters had not started any big work, that they were doing small things quietly, I said that even if they helped only one person, that was all right; Jesus would have died for one person, for one sinner.

The Minister of the Imperial Court in Addis Ababa asked a few searching questions:

"What do you want from the Government?"

"Nothing, I have only come to offer my Sisters to work among the poor suffering people."

"What will your Sisters do?"

"We give wholehearted free service to the poorest of the poor."

"What qualifications do they have?"

"We try to bring tender love and compassion to the unwanted, to the unloved."

"Do you preach to the people, trying to convert them?"

"Our works of love reveal to the suffering poor the love of God for them."

You have a welfare state in England, but I have walked at night and gone into your homes and found people dying unloved. Here you have a different kind of poverty—a poverty of the spirit, of loneliness, and of being unwanted. And that is the worst disease in the world today, not tuberculosis or leprosy. I think England needs more and more for the people to know who the poor are. People in England should give their hearts to love the poor, and also their hands to serve them. And they cannot do that unless they know them, and knowledge will lead them to love, and love to service.

In England and other places, in Calcutta, in Melbourne, in New York, we find lonely people who are known by the number of their room. Why are we not there? Do we really know that there are some people, maybe next-door to us? Maybe there is a blind man who would be happy if you would read the newspaper for him; maybe there is a rich person who has no one to visit him—he has plenty of other things, he is nearly drowned in them, but there is not that touch and he needs your touch. Some time back a very rich man came to our place, and he said to me: "Please, either you or somebody, come to my house. I am nearly half-blind and my wife is nearly mental; our children have all gone abroad, and we are dying of loneliness, we are longing for the loving sound of a human voice."

Let us not be satisfied with just giving money. Money is not enough, money can be got, but they need your hearts to love them. So, spread love everywhere you go: first of all in your own home. Give love to your children, to your wife or husband, to a next-door neighbor.

❖

You ask how I should see the task of the Missionaries of Charity if I were a religious sister or priest in Surrey or Sussex. Well, the task of the Church in such places is much more difficult than what we face in Calcutta, Yemen, or anywhere else, where all the people need is dressing for their wounds, a bowl of rice and a "cuddle," with someone telling them they are loved and wanted. In Surrey and Sussex the problems of your people are deep down, at the bottom of their hearts. They have to come to know you and trust you, to see you as a person with Christ's compassion and love, before their problems will emerge and you can help them. This takes a lot of time! Time for you to be people of prayer and time to give of yourself to each one of your people.

WILLING SLAVES TO THE WILL OF GOD

"Thou shalt love the Lord thy God with thy whole heart, with thy whole soul, and with thy whole mind." This is the commandment of the great God, and he cannot command the impossible. Love is a fruit in season at all times, and within reach of every hand. Anyone may gather it and no limit is set. Everyone can reach this love through meditation, spirit of prayer, and sacrifice, by an intense inner life.

There is no limit, because God is love and

love is God, and so you are really in love with God. And then, God's love is infinite. But part is to love and to give until it hurts. And that's why it's not how much you do, but how much love you put into the action. How much love we put in our presents. That's why people—maybe they are very rich people—who have not got a capacity to give and to receive love are the poorest of the poor. And I think this is what our Sisters have got—the spreading of joy that you see in many religious people who have given themselves without reserve to God.

Our work is only the expression of the love we have for God. We have to pour our love on someone, and the people are the means of expressing our love for God.

We need to find God, and he cannot be found

in noise and restlessness. God is the friend of silence. See how nature—trees, flowers, grass—grows in silence; see the stars, the moon, and the sun, how they move in silence. Is not our mission to give God to the poor in the slums? Not a dead God, but a living, loving God. The more we receive in silent prayer, the more we can give in our active life. We need silence to be able to touch souls. The essential thing is not what we say, but what God says to us and through us. All our words will be useless unless they come from within; words that do not give the light of Christ increase the darkness.

To show great love for God and our neighbor we need not do great things. It is how much love we put in the doing that makes our offering Something Beautiful for God.

The great hindrance to us in our work is that we are not yet saints; that we cannot spread to the full the love of Christ. That is what distresses us most when we travel.

St. Teresa of Avila? Oh no! I haven't called myself after the big Teresa, but after the little one, Teresa of Lisieux.

✤

Our progress in holiness depends on God and ourselves—on God's grace and on our will to be holy. We must have a real living determination to reach holiness. "I will be a saint" means I will despoil myself of all that is not God; I will strip my heart of all created things; I will live in poverty and detachment; I will renounce my will, my inclinations, my whims and fancies, and make myself a willing slave to the will of God.

LOVE TO PRAY

Make us worthy, Lord, to serve our fellowmen throughout the world who live and die in poverty and hunger. Give them, through our hands, this day their daily bread, and by our understanding love, give peace and joy.

Dearest Lord, may I see you today and every day in the person of your sick, and, whilst nursing them, minister unto you. Though you hide yourself behind the unattractive disguise of the irritable, the exacting, the unreasonable, may I still recognize you, and say: "Jesus, my patient, how sweet it is to serve you."

Lord, give me this seeing faith; then my work will never be monotonous. I will ever find joy in humoring the fancies and gratifying the wishes of all poor sufferers.

O beloved sick, how doubly dear you are to me when you personify Christ; and what a privilege is mine to be allowed to tend you.

Sweetest Lord, make me appreciative of the dignity of my high vocation, and its many responsibilities. Never permit me to disgrace it by giving way to coldness, unkindness, or impatience.

And, O God, while you are Jesus, my pa-

72

tient, deign also to be to me a patient Jesus, bearing with my faults, looking only to my intention, which is to love and serve you in the person of each of your sick. Lord, increase my faith, bless my efforts and work, now and forevermore.

Lord, help us to see in your crucifixion and resurrection an example of how to endure and seemingly to die in the agony and conflict of daily life, so that we may live more fully and creatively. You accepted patiently and humbly the rebuffs of human life, as well as the tortures of your crucifixion and passion. Help us to accept the pains and conflicts that come to us each day as opportunities to grow as people and become more like you. Enable us to go through them patiently and bravely, trusting that you will support us. Make us realize that it is only by frequent deaths of ourselves and our self-centered desires that we can come to live more fully; for it is only by dying with you that we can rise with you.

It is not possible to engage in the direct apostolate without being a soul of prayer. We must be aware of oneness with Christ, as he was aware of oneness with his Father. Our activity is truly apostolic only insofar as we permit him to work in us and through us with his power, with his desire, with his love.

We must become holy, not because we want to feel holy, but because Christ must be able to live his life fully in us. We are to be all love, all faith, all purity, for the sake of the poor we serve. And once we have learned to seek God and his will, our contacts with the poor will become the means of great sanctity to ourselves and to others.

Love to pray. Feel often during the day the need for prayer, and take trouble to pray. Prayer enlarges the heart until it is capable of containing God's gift of himself. Ask and seek, and your heart will grow big enough to receive him and keep him as your own.

Let us all become a true and fruitful branch on the vine Jesus, by accepting him in our lives as it pleases him to come:

> as the Truth—to be told;
> as the Life—to be lived;
> as the Light—to be lighted;
> as the Love—to be loved;
> as the Way—to be walked;
> as the Joy—to be given;

as the Peace—to be spread;

as the Sacrifice—to be offered,

in our families and our neighbors.

In Holy Communion we have Christ under the appearance of bread. In our work we find him under the appearance of flesh and blood. It is the same Christ.

The Mass is the spiritual food that sustains me, without which I could not get through one single day or hour in my life; in the Mass we have Jesus in the appearance of bread, while in the slums we see Christ and touch him in the broken bodies, in the abandoned children.

JOY

Joy is prayer; joy is strength; joy is love; joy is a net of love by which you can catch souls. God loves a cheerful giver. She gives most who gives with joy. The best way to show our gratitude to God and the people is to accept everything with joy. A joyful heart is the inevitable result of a heart burning with love. Never let anything so fill you with sorrow as to make you forget the joy of the Christ risen.

We all long for heaven where God is, but

we have it in our power to be in heaven with him right now—to be happy with him at this very moment. But being happy with him now means:

loving as he loves,
helping as he helps,
giving as he gives,
serving as he serves,
rescuing as he rescues,
being with him for all the twenty-four
    hours,
touching him in his distressing dis-
    guise.